SEA BETWEEN

WORDS BY JESSICA COTTEN
DESIGN BY JAMIE HARRIS

PUBLISHED BY LUNARIA PUBLISHING
SEA BETWEEN © 2019 JESSICA COTTEN

jessicacotten.com

ISBN: 978-1-7336486-0-8

SEA BETWEEN

a collection

JESSICA COTTEN

ONE

TWO

THREE

ONE

THE CRACKS, THE CLOUDS, THE FACES

in the dappled sunlight
  of a new dawn
i mostly feel hope,
  the chance to try again
          fight again
          learn again.
the light draws me in.

but,
a frayed and fractured humanity
arises.
and we collide.

i don't want to be a robot;
i won't.

i find my solace
in letting go,
shining on
the cracks, the clouds, the faces.
steady,
like the light.

WE RESTED BENEATH

Under a blanket of ebony,
a magnetic voice
pulled us through.
We were free.

Family of fire,
sojourners of skies,
companions to darkness
once absent, now alive.

Faceless
we flicker
in circular
motion.

Weightless
we wander;
our pilgrimage
chosen by time.

Like ribbons
tied to eternity,
time is a sacred rescue.
Driven forward to
a bright destiny.

We, the called forth
We, the glimmering roar
We, the glow makers
Silent no more.

SEA BETWEEN

The sea between
You and me,
I will cross,
Fix the distance,
Meet me there
In the depths
In between
I can hear you
Love is stronger
Than this rift
We will make it,
We will give
Ourselves to each other
Ourselves to the sea.

WORKING IT OUT

"Let's talk awhile," she said, looking at me with eyes that could see deep down inside of me. No judgment. Just an invitation to let it out in the safety of good company.

We walked for hours. Stepping across rocks and striding across fields, wading through tall grasses, and trekking up hills. Her friendship meant the world to me that day. I knew I could trust her. She didn't mind if I babbled. She didn't insert her struggles into the conversation.

Not many people will just listen like she did that day.

"I thought it would work. I followed my instincts and did the right thing every time. I made mature decisions. I made myself low to get in touch with the pain. I tried to get better. I made myself available for a renovation. Nothing has worked..."

I told her, and then I stopped and let it hang in the air.

"I don't think I can try again. I don't trust the voice that led me here."

Her gaze never stopped holding me.

"What if you just waited?" she asked.

"I don't know what that even means," I said quietly, studying the texture of the grasses beneath my feet as we walked.

It didn't sound difficult, the way she said it. Sometimes waiting is tedious and gut wrenching. This time it felt possible.

We walked further, and I continued to talk. It felt good.

Sometimes working it out means making a decision. Sometimes it means exercise. Sometimes it means drinking. Moving. Changing.

Sometimes it means walking with a good friend who knows you well, and affirms your existence by extending an invitation for you to just talk.

THE WAY OF THE BRAVE

The way of the brave
Is often unseen;
Like treasure,
Hidden beneath
A muddy sea.

Dive! Dive! Dive!
Dive deep!
Hands sweep away
the dirt and debris.

The veil between real and false
Thin, like air.

Swim through the veil,
Swim fast.

This route is for
The brave.
This route is for
You.

The treasure awaits.
The treasure is real.
It is open to
The way of the brave.

TWO

TO BE BORN

What will we witness
At the end of this tunnel,
This burrowed darkness

These echoing voices

What is to be born
From such a fierce
And trying labor

The unlit path
Before us
A shadow
Like skin on our hands
Stuck to us
A part of us

Grey skies
Never part;
Dim glow,
Hidden

But we
The blind
Will see.

FROM HERE TO THERE

If I walk where you go, there will be thorns.
They will pierce the soles of my feet. You said
you'd always step first. I may be a pioneer
among some, but not with you. You've been
everywhere. Your journeys mystify me. When
I complain about the thorns, you empathize.
And you keep walking...

You're my favorite mountain guide. I'm
learning to follow you even when it hurts.
After the thorny path comes a clearing with
a vista, always. Your guidebook promised me
that. I always forget.

I'd like to not curse you anymore. I don't think
you guide people on immense treks unless
you think that they are immense themselves.
You have a certain way about you, dear
mountain guide, of affirming a strength in me
that I cannot see. Oh, your ways are baffling.

I like your mystery. And I like myself as seen
through your eyes.

MERCY, FIGHT

We can fight for the truth without fighting for payback.

Yes, it is possible.

We can fight for equality without slandering those who
have enslaved us.

Yes, it is possible.

We can be honest without sounding hopeless.

Yes, it is possible.

We can stand for justice without being driven by revenge.

Yes, it is possible.

Truth rides on wings of mercy

A deliberate voyage

Soon appearing on the horizon

Prepare the way.

THE HAWK AND I

There's a hawk flying.
What does he see?
He does not perceive,
But he does see.
Creatures, crowds
Movements, objects
Stillness, turbulence

Assorted occurrences.
The hawk sees.
I perceive.

In the midst of a frenzy
I see
The hawk is silent.
Should I be?
I perceive
My words
To be
Weapons.
Of good use,
Of abuse;
For disarming,
For harming.

There's a hawk flying overhead.
The hawk sees.
I see.

OUR HAVEN IS A BRIGHT STAR

The lies of winter are upon us. We must flee them.

Where we go is a mystery. Our haven is a bright star, which warms our hearts and guides our way. We will not succumb to the lies of winter. Though they lure and they beckon and call, they do not match the fire of our star.

The lies of winter run deep beneath the ground, growing roots to tangle our feet. Their branches suffocate us with emptiness, and take the brilliance of color away. They surround us with the heaviness of gray. They trap us in a permanent embrace.

The lies of winter are that desolation and death are forever. And every year, we feel them trying to wrap their mangled arms around us, promising us harm.

If it were not for our bright star, steady in the morning and faithful in the evening, we would perish in the lies of winter. Our star, brilliant and safe, alive and strong, is our security that there is something beyond.

Our star breaks through the gray. We grab hold of it, believing in its ability to outshine and outlast the suffocation of our present, and in it we are safe, we are home, we are at rest.

Winter may scream at us day and night. It may tell us stories of darkness, loneliness, sadness, and danger. But our haven is a bright star. And we hold tight.

HAIKU

We hold each other
Ears close enough to listen
Prejudice leaves

Outdated labels
Bow before our true essence
Equal, you and I

MEND MY SIGHT

Rid me of my misperceptions.

Take from me

My tendency

To know you with conditions.

Remove the stain of inhibitions,
Free my thinking from its caged intuition.

I am too small.

My mind is too closed.

And I want to fly

Through this course, crusty wall
Built by edicts,
By judgements,
And critics.

I see you, in flight.

Take me there,

Mend my sight.

FORGOTTEN EMBER

stars shine
and so do I.
if it's dark,
there's a light.
there has to be.
Right?
Maybe
  it's
            me.

I hold the light.

THREE

THE SOUND OUTSIDE

There. My ears perked.

In a moment, my entire world shifted. I heard something.

There it is again. I recognized this sound.

I breathed slowly. My heart rate calmed. I had suddenly entered into clear thinking.

All because of a sound.

The dirt of this world left me. The gritty endeavors of this culture washed off of me, and I felt a strange sensation rise up to take over. Relief.

All because of hearing this sound.

I didn't feel so alone. I felt surrounded by family. I could not see them, but my ears felt the sound of home.

And what was the sound? The sound that rushed in and changed everything?

Birds. Singing their way through the day.

Tiny creatures. Voices that heal. They reminded me to slow down, to not worry, to be content.

And here they were again, faithful to offer me another worthwhile escape. I just had to step outside.

Outside, we learn from the birds, that sing songs that we don't understand.

But they are songs we need to hear.

STONE STEPS

An arduous climb
A steep ascent
Aching bones
Weary soul
I thought the adversity
Would do me in.
Who would carry me?

What I found
Instead
Strength beneath my feet
Swirling to me, around me
Inside me

Like breath

Like water

A sudden catalyst
A gentle incitement
I can embrace this help

This way.

TO RISE

I want to rise, in my weariness
to touch the air
through flight.

Moving on
Moving up
Moving o v e r
Moving through

To be grounded is to die,
When you were made to fly.
Some prefer feet fixed
In earth
But I am from another world,
Where flying
Comes first.

Surrendering to ground
I am pulled
By force.
Surrendering to fly
I am pulled
By mystery.

Surrender is
Easier
When talked about,
Not done.

IMPOSTER

Everyone wants to feel important
Everyone wants to feel safe
The quickest way you got there
Is by being on the stage.

"Show me your great works!"
"Your acts, your strengths, your deeds!"
"Put them on stage for all of us to see!"

The crowd goes wild
Chants with glee
As you tell us
Of your menageries.

Then, halfway through your rousing, dashing speech
I realize you're pretending;
Lying through your teeth.
Those things you do
And say with ease?
Recycled words
Carried by the breeze;
Heard elsewhere,
Someone else's dream.

You've nothing more than magic
Tricks
To help you with your power
Kicks.

You're nothing but a mouth;
Fabricating acts

Unscathed.

BRIGHT EYES

The brightness of your spirit,
Hold on to it.
Hold on to your light.

And know you are worthy of greatness.
Love is greatness.

Rivers of temptation to imitate
will be pushed
By your light,
  your love,
  your eyes.

You are a field of wildflowers
In a world of manicured lawns.

THE WIND WILL CARRY

"I remember the day you were born," she said.

The comment caught me off guard. I never realized she had been present at my birth. I knew her as my friend, and not as my parents' friend.

I had never stopped to think about when we met, or how we met. She had just always… been. Sometimes I called her, sometimes she called me. She simply had always been there for me, without me really understanding how.

"When you cried out that first time," she said, looking off into the hills like they were holding a picture of the memory, "I said, 'Oh, now this one here… this one will change the world with her voice.'"

My thoughts paused. I listened. Tears started to form around my eyes as I realized how much I meant to her. Sometimes you just need to hear how much you matter.

"I know what you're thinking," she told me. "You're thinking we say that to everyone."

I looked straight at her. Yes. That was what I was thinking.

"We don't." Her gaze never left mine.

(Never mind the "we." I knew what she meant. There were more just like her, companions and encouragers.)

I thought I was going to burst open. Part of me wanted to argue, "Yes, you do say that to everyone! I've heard it from their own mouths!"

And then, the wind. Oh, the wind. It started to blow.

Moving gently and slowly at first, it spread through the leaves of every tree, touching the grass across the fields, sweeping through our surroundings like a symphony sweeps through a concert hall. It grew and it grew and it grew, getting louder and stronger. Some leaves shook and fell to the ground, some held on for dear life. I felt the wind around me like a blanket. It carried a message, this wind burst.

I sighed. I breathed in deeply. There was something in the wind for me to take in. So I took it. I stopped and lay down on the ground. I didn't want to miss anything in that moment. The wind was endorsing her words.

I closed my eyes and considered her being right. I remembered that she usually is right. Never in a proud way. It's one of the reasons I valued her friendship so much.

"My voice. It's important." I said aloud, mostly to remind myself of what was happening.

The words were simple. Most profound things are.

"Help me to not forget the story of when I was born," I asked her.

Sometimes I feel like a little child all over again with her. She never shames me for it.

I wish everyone knew that the wind carried messages.

44

LIKE WIND LIKE SPIRIT

I will surround you
Like wind, like spirit
Encircling and enveloping
While you let go

Of the day, of the fights,
Of the weariness, the lies.

In this place of safety
There is rest.
Look for this. It will be here for you.

And hear the voice
It says: Acceptance.
Pure love. Security.
Open arms.

Follow the peace.

Home is here.

O LIGHT, COME QUICKLY

Dusk,
Trying to hide me;
I run,
Shadows find me.
Darkness disperses,
I cannot escape,
But dawn
Is on
The way.

O light, come quickly;
Reach into the depths of me.
Darkness says
It will vacate you.
You say
It's making room
For you.

Night, trying to
Beat me
Reduce me
Kill me.

Light, coming to
Wake me
Save me
Clean me.

I cling
To light.
I survive
The night.

Dusk to dawn,
How strong the light!
Even in darkness
Freedom takes flight.

LOVE STARTS TO RETURN

Once, you gave us a gift.
A work of art, unique and special.
We loved it, back then.

We lost sight of the gift, of its beauty.
We forgot what you said.
Love, your love, disappeared from our memory.

But sometimes, when the wind blows,
we start to remember.
We hear the dolphins sing,
we start to remember.
The sun rises,
spreading its reflection in colors
we could never dream up ourselves,
and we start to remember.

Caterpillars are reborn,
flowers unfurl,
birds take flight,
leaves cast themselves off of trees
And we remember.

The land we once loved,
Given to us again.
The giver of the gift,
Calling to us again.

We remember
what it means to belong,
and we remember our charge:
Make a home for all.

ABOUT THE AUTHOR

Jessica Cotten lives in central Pennsylvania. She has a B.A. in Spanish and International Relations, a certificate in Intelligence Collection, and a certificate in Herbalism. She values variety and craves change. Her favorite season is Spring, her days usually include playing music and roaming the hillsides, and her heart is almost always on a tropical island. She really likes tacos.

Her current writing endeavors are focused on poetry and a sci-fi/speculative fantasy series set to release in 2020. She maintains an online journal of poems, sayings, and imaginary conversations with imaginary people, which can be perused at jessicacotten.com. Stay in touch! She likes you.